Recollections of

A CAPE COD MARINER

An american citizen, captured by a french frigate in the high seas, requests a personal interview, & to lay his grievances before citizen Robespierre. very respectfully

E. Cobb

In about an hour, I received the following note, in his own hand writing.

I will grant citizen Cobb an interview to morrow at 10 A.M.

Robespierre.

This, gave a spring to my feelings, and banished that despair which had held me in chains for some days previous. I was punctual to the time — sent my name up, & was admitted into the presence of the great man. He pointed me to a seat without speaking; there was one man only, in the Hall, an interpreter, who told me that, citizen Robespierre wished me to commence my relation, at the time of my capture, and to tell the whole, up to this time — I accordingly proceeded; and, thro' the interpreter, related my capture & treatment, up to that time — upon my closing the detail; with a wave of Robespierre's hand, the interpreter left the Hall, and he, R——, began conversing

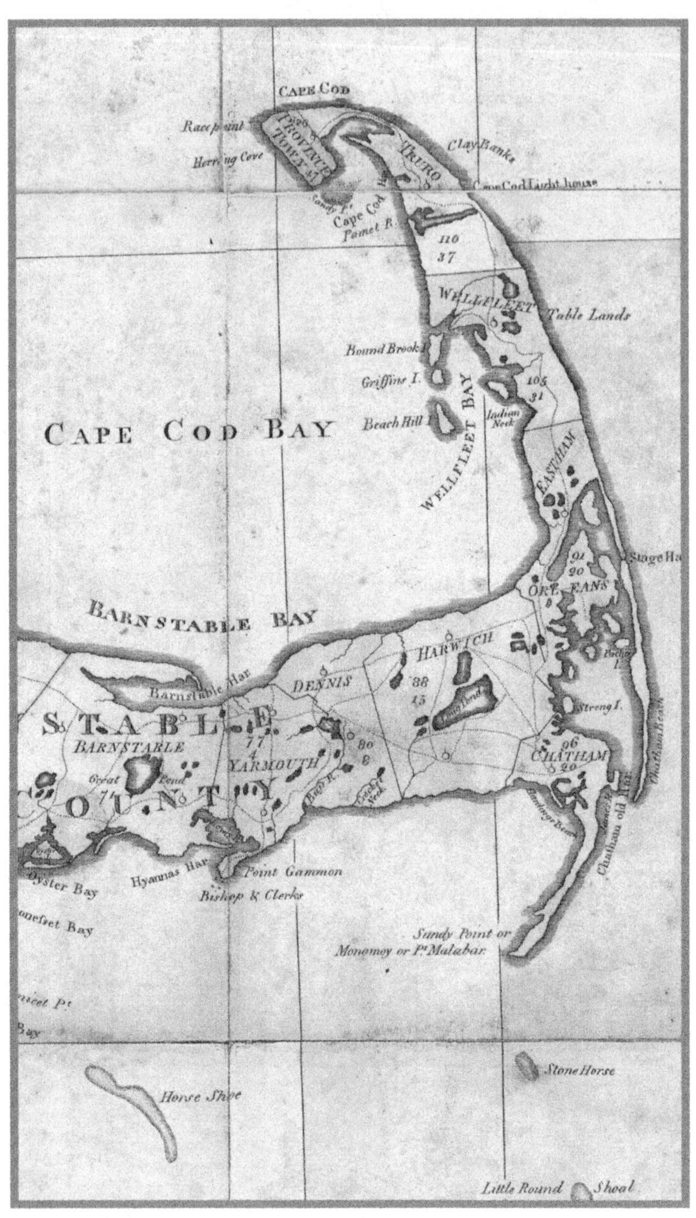

Cape Cod Bay, 1801.

Recollections of
A CAPE COD MARINER

Elijah Cobb, 1768–1848

EDITED BY DEBORAH HILL

NORTH ROAD
PUBLISHING

EDITOR'S NOTE

Elijah Cobb's Recollections were written 170 years ago, just at the time Webster's dictionary was published. The captain, then 75 years old, was clearly unaffected by this event. His spelling is inventive and phonetic and is, in my opinion, part of the charm of his memoir. Occasionally it causes some doubt about the meaning of one word or another. In such cases I have applied some judicious tinkering in the interest of clarity. I can only hope I've done so accurately.

Cobb's liberal use of commas was easier to resolve. I eliminated most of them, for they occur at every fifth word or so, causing the reader, to pause unnecessarily, again, and again and, again. I've removed many of the semi-colons that Cobb customarily used in conjunction with "&". I left italicized words as I found them, thinking that perhaps they were underlined in the original manuscript.

A more delicate matter is Cobb's composition. He often grouped several ideas together, instead of breaking them into separate sentences or paragraphs. This makes it difficult to follow the action he describes. Then there is the matter of awkward or ungrammatical expression that tends to be challenging to the reader. How much can be changed without losing Cobb's individuality? I decided: as little as possible. If the reader has to work a bit harder, I think the flavor retained is worth the effort.

Cobb's recollections were edited by Ralph D. Paine in 1925 under the auspices of Yale University. Paine wrote a fine introduction which explains the historical background of Cobb's adventures. I think it's helpful for the reader to be conversant with these events, for they are responsible for many of the Captain's escapades. To understand them and keep them straight (they *are* complicated!) I'd personally recommend reading my novel, *This is the House*, which is based on this memoir and uses the facts as a background drum-roll.

I have included a few notes, in order to clarify some specifics and a few dates that don't quite agree with history as we know it today. Cobb was old when he wrote this memoir, and a mistaken date is understandable.

Paine's edition, by the way, is still available on Amazon. It includes copies of letters that the captain wrote when he ran into trouble off the African coast after the War of 1812, and a few to his son Elijah, as well as a very pleasant note written by his grandson telling of Cobb's life in retirement. But the captain wrote nothing more about his career after describing his capture by the British, and concludes his Recollections with a well-described homecoming. And that, in my opinion, is the perfect place to stop.

Deborah Hill

CONTENTS

The following
is committed to paper for
the Gratification and
amusement of my beloved
Grand-Children

Elijah Cobb

CHAPTER

EARLY YEARS

My mother was only 12 years old when her Father died. At 17 she married my Father, Scottow Cobb. My Father pursued a sea-faring life for subsistence. He was Master of a Brig, & died on his passage from Cadiz to Quebec in the 33d year of his age, leaving my Mother with 6 infant children, the oldest but 10 years of age, and the youngest, born after Father left home the last time.

For the support of this helpless flock was a small cape cod farm, a small house & barn, and one cow. I have heard my Mother say, that she never received $100 for my Father's effects. Under such circumstances it was not possible to keep the family together. To support & educate us with the means in her power was out of the question. Some of us must leave the perternal dwelling & seek subsistence among strangers. My Bro, being the Elder, was tried first, but wou'd not stay, & came home crying. I was then in my 6th year, & although too young to earn my living, I left my dear mother for that subsistence among strangers which she could not procure for me.

This is called a "half-house" and Elijah's family very likely lived in a similar one. It was the standard model when Cobb's grandfather came to Brewster, then known as Harwich. There aren't many of them left; this one is dated 1720.

I continued from my Mother except at times visiting her until in my 13th year, when by an imprudent attempt to lift beyond my strength, I broke a vessell in my stomack, which entirely disenabled me. I was sent home, incapable of labour of any kind.

I remained with my mother, under the care of a skilfull Docter, for about a year, when he advised that I be sent to sea as the best method to regain my health. Accordingly, in the fall of 1783, I was fitted out for Boston, to look for a voyage. My whole wardrobe was packed in a gin case for a trunk; a tow bed-sack, filled with rye straw, & a pair of home made blankets for sleeping appuratis, with two bushels of corn to pay my passage to Boston—and acquipted thus, I left the family circle, with buoyant sperits and in full confidence that I should work myself thro life, with honour & credit—

I embarked at Skaket in a small Schooner of only 25 Tons called the *Creture*, & after going into Provincetown & laying there during a gale of

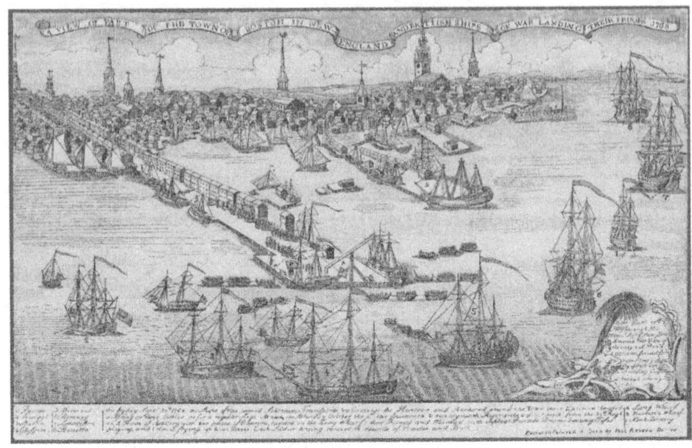

A view of the Town of Boston in New England and British ships of war landing their troops, 1768 (Source: http://flickr.com/photos/24029425@ N06/2885434574/ Boston Public Library). The city would not have changed much, if at all, by the time Cobb arrived there fifteen years later.

wind, we reached Boston in 3 days. At the time I am speaking of there were more men than could readily find employ. Frequently the best of seamen were distitute of voyages. Several of our neighbouring young men had been to Boston that fall, previous to my leaving home, & had returned without giting employ. They told my Mother that I would only spend the two bushels of corn, & return to her without giting a voyage—but their predictions were set at naught, for the first time I went down the long wharf & stood gazeing at a new vessell, wondering, & admiring her monstrous size, her great cables & anchors &c, a gentleman stept from her deck & thus accosted me:

"My lad, do you want a voyage?"

"Yes Sir!"

"Will you go with me in this vessell?"

"Where are you bound, Sir?"

"To Siranam."

"I am told Sir, that all flesh die, that go there."

"Well my boy, to prove that you have not been told the truth, I have been there 13 voyages, & you see I'm alive yet."

"Well Sir, I should like to go. What wages will you allow me?"

"Do you know how to cook?"

"Not much Sir, but I can soon learn."

"Well, my boy, if you think so, I presume you will. I like your candour & will take you & give you the customary wages of a boy: half of Seamens wages $3.50* per month, but you must go immediately on board, & git dinner for the men at work."

Thus I commenced my duty as cook & cabin Boy. When the men broke off work, at night, they all went away. The Capt. then asked me where my bed & cloaths were. I told him, on board the *creture*, in town dock.

"Well, you must go & git them, & I'll keep ship untill you return. You must sleep on board to night."

"Who else will sleep on board?"

"Nobody, there is no one belongs to the vessell, except you & myself."

Not liking the idea of sleeping on board alone, I took the liberty of asking him where his mate

---

*About $32 in today's dollars. That would have seemed huge in a community using corn for cash.

was. He said he had not got one yet. I told him, I *gessed* I knew a good man, that would like to go.

"Who is he?"

"My Uncle, who came up in the *creture* to look for a voyage."

"Has he ever been mate?"

"Yes Sir, & prise mastre too, in the war."

"Well, you go after your things, & if you see your Uncle, ask him to come down & see me in the morning."

When I got on board the *creture*, my Uncle was there, and by way of a reprimand, asked, where I had been all day. "Why Uncle", said I, "I have shipped myself, & I beleive I have got a voyage for you also."

To make a short story, my Uncle went down in the morning, & shipped on the voyage. I then wrote to my Mother that I had got a voyage for myself & Uncle, & if those young men would come to

Boston before I sailed, I would ship them off, too, rather than have them stay at home Idle all winter.

The vessell was soon loaded, & we went to sea. My inexperienc, & being very sea-sick for a while, rendered my situation very unpleasant, but I soon surmounted those deficulties & began to injoy my new mode of life. After the opperation of David Jones's medecine (sea-sickness) I felt my health improved, & by the time we arrived in Surinam, I felt quite well, and I found I was able to give pritty good satisfaction in my line of duty. My perticular attention to the officers procured me some presents, by which I was enabled to purchase a Barrel of molasses & some fruit for an adventure back to Boston.

Nothing meterial worth noting took place during the remainder of the voyage; we returned to Boston in the spring of 1784, discharged our cargo, mollases, was paid our wages & seperated, each to home. My wages amouted to 21$, & by the sale of my bbl of Molases & some of my fruit, I was enabled to git myself a new suit of sailors cloaths from the Slopshop, & carried home &

put into my Mothers hands, 20 silver Dollars—
probably the largest sum of money she had pos-
sesd since she had been a widow, & that from her
poor little sick Boy. Her tears flowed freely upon
the occasion, but they were tears of gratitude to
our heavenly Father, for his mercies to her child
in permitting his return home in so much better
health than he left it. My own feelings, upon the
occasion, can be better imagined than discribed.

I tarried at home but a short time before I
returned to Boston in persuit of employ & spent
the summer, with a Capt. Lombard, in the coast-
ing business. In the fall I shipped as a common
sailor & made several voyages to the W. Indies.

Returning from a voyage in December 1786, I
was informed that my Brother had fallen from
mast-head in the Delaware Bay, had Broken both
his legs, one thigh, put out of joint one shoul-
der and was then in the Pensalvinia hospital, with
one leg amputated. The Season was then so far
advanced, that the navigation was about closing
with Ice. Consequently, I was compelled to relin-
quish my visit to my unfortunate Brother untill
the spring opened the navigation.

Prehaps you will ask: why G'd Father did not go on by land? But, my dear G. children, the mode of traveling then was quite different from now. We had no railroads, no steam conveyance, and scarcly a carriage. Even the mail was carried upon horses—a stage coach was not known.

I consequently engaged a birth for the spring, with my uncle John Cobb, in the employ of Benjamin Cobb & Sons, of Boston, in the Philadelphia trade. I went home & attended School, for about 2 months, when I was call'd upon to go on to Boston by land to join the vessell.

I accordingly started in company with 3 others & walked to Boston. We there joined the vessell, loaded her, & saild for Philadelphia. On our arrival, I procured a permit as soon as posible & visited my poor Brother in the hospital. Affectionate Brothers & Sisters can better imagine our feelings at meeting than I can describe.

Suffice it to say he was not well enough to leave the hospital then, but t'was thought he wou'd be by our next trip which only took about a month.

Accordingly, the next time he came with us to Boston & I sent him home to our Mother.

I continued in the employ of B.C. & Sons about a year when they premoted me to the office of mate. In that capacity I served them under many different captains, between 6 & 7 years until I felt myself qualified to command a vessel. Seeing no disposition on their part to indulge me, I left their employ, went to Baltimore, & made two voyages to Europe in the capacity of 1st mate of a ship—after which I returned to Boston and got the command of a Brig in the employ of Edwd & William Reynolds. After making several voyages to Virginia & one to the West Indies, I went to the cape in April, 1793, and got married. I was then in my 25th year.

CHAPTER

2

ADVENTURES
IN FRANCE

I continued in the employ of the Messrs. Reynolds's about two years longer, principally in the virginia trade, when they concluded to send me on a voyage to Europe. Their object was Cadiz, but at that time the algerines were at war with America, and it was reported that their crusiers were outside of the streights of Gibaralter.* In consequence, it was recommended that I should clear my vessell for Curruna, a north-

*Moslem pirates in the Mediterranean made trade with Spain hazardous. America paid annual tribute to protect her merchant traders, with only limited success. The American navy was created in order to deal forcibly with this problem, but no formal war was declared until 1801. Cobb's reference to "the algerines" being "at war" with the United States describes the state of affairs in 1794, when the actions of the Barbary pirates were definitelty war-like.

ern port in Spain, and there essertain whether it would be safe to proceed to Cadiz.

I was, however, spared the trouble of enquirry by falling in with a French Frigate, who capturd & sent me to France, & here commenced my first trouble & anxiety as a ship Master, having under my charge a valuable vessell & cargo, inexperienced in business—carried into a foreign port, and unacquainted with the language, no American consel or merchant to advise with— and my reputation as a ship master depending upon the measures I persued &c.

The time that I arrived in France was during the french Revolution, and in the *bloody* reign of Robertspeire. All was arnachy & confusion, the galliotine in continual operation, their streets & publick squars drenched with human blood. I noted down 1000 persons that I saw beheaded by that *infernal* machine, and probably saw as many more that I did not note down—men, women, preists & laymen of all ages and finally, before I left the country, I saw Robertspeirs head taken off by the same Machine—

But to return to my induvidual and embari-sed affairs. All my papers relative to my ship & voyage had been taken from me on board the Frigate at sea. I concluded they were put in possession of the prise Master who brought me in, but he was not to be found; neither could I find any clue to my papers, and without them, I could not prove any demand for redress upon the government for their violation of our neu-trality. It was true my vessel was there, but her cargo of Flour & Rice had been taken out & was daily made into bread, soups, &c &c, for the half starved populace. Without papers I could not even substanciate my claim to an empty ship. They condecended to send me to a Hotell to board. Those of my ships crew that were sent in with me were also provided for.

In this very unpleasant perdicerment I remained about six weeks. I had, however, in that time, written to the american charge des affairs at Paris & received an answer, but it contained noth-ing definite. He regreted my situation & that of my countrymen generally in France, which was owing to the disorganized state of affairs in the country, and that I must exercise patiance & the government would do what was right, in time.

In about six weeks, as before observed, I was called upon at my lodgings by an officer of the tribunal of commerce, bringing a copy of the judgment of said tribunal upon my vessel and cargo, & a linguister to explain it to me.

Thus, had they tried me & passed sentence without my hearing, or even knowing that I was on trial—but in that way all business was managed in France at that time.

The decision of the tribunal was, however, so favourable that it gave a spring to my feelings, & a sensation of new life. They declared my vessell & cargo to be (newtrial*) property & that, as the cargo was at my disposition, I should be paid for it by the government at prices that might be fixed upon by myself & the agent of the government, and an adequate endemnification for my capture, detention, expenditures &c &c.

____

*neutral

I was then waited upon by an agent of marine to sell my cargo. It was presumed that there was not a pound of the flour or rice in existence. After battleing in words, three days in succession, we fixed the prices as follows, viz—Flour $16.50, & Rice $5.50. This was a good begining, being over 200 prcent on the invoice.

But a long altercation now insue'd relative to the payment. Money was out of the question, for even if they had it to pay, there was a law against bringing it away from the country. Goods, also, were out of the question, as well as bills on England or America. Finally I agreed to take government Bills of exchange* on Hamburg, payable 60 days after date, and was promised by the Agent that I should have my bills in 12 or 14 days.

I waited patiently a month, but no bills came, & finding that no confidence could be placed in their promises, & feeling doubtful as to obtaining anything for my Cargo, I thought it advisable to send my vessell home, under charge of the

---

*Bills of exchange are similar to checks and promissory notes. They are transferable and can bind one party to pay a third party that was not involved in its creation. (investopedia.com/)

mate. Consequently, I ballased her & sent her away, writing to my owners that I was determind to persevere untill I obtained satisfaction.

My mind being releived from seing my vessell laying Idle and at great expense, I came to the determination to go to headquarters in Paris, but many deficulties were to be surmounted in order to attain this object. The road was dangerous to travail; the adherents of royalty were reduced to mere scurmaging parties that commited their depradations under cover of the night, in solitary places upon both travellers & the peaceble inhabitants.

All horses had been taken into requisition by the government, except those that conveyd national dispatches. There was no other mode of travelling, and it was conterary to law for the mail couriers to take passengers, but my mind was fixed upon going as the only chance of ever accomplishing my business with the French government.

I therefore called upon the Minister of Marine & got an official copy of my demands on the government and had them recorded (a precautionary measure, as I had learned that loseing a man's papers was one of their methods of procrastination, thus keeping a settlement far off.) After this, I procured an interpreter & waited upon Jean Con. St. Andre, a man holding high offices under the Government & reported to be favourably disposed to Americans.

To him I made known my situation—the treatment I had received, the perplexity I was in & the necessity of going to Paris & praying him not only to grant me a passport, but to grant a special permitt to one of the mail Coureirs to carry me there. After a long demur, & repeatedly feeling of his neck to see how it would bear the knife, he returned a favourable reply—viz. that I must call upon him the next day, when he would make the necessary arrangments &c.

Accordingly, in two days, I was underway for Paris with one of the national coureirs carrying government dispatches, the Master of which did not speak one word of English & myself but a few words of French, so we were not very sociable. We were each furnished with a pair of pistals, and a loaded blunderbuss in front. (Our carraige was musquet-shot proof, except in front). We drove with a postilion outside with from 5 to 9 horses, depending on the road which, at best, was very indifferent. Thus we drove on, Jehu like, without stopping except to exchange horses & mail, taking occasionally, as we ran, a mouthfull of bread and washing it down with some low priced, red Burgendy wine. As to sleep, I did not git one wink during the journey of 684 miles. But *la maitre de les despach* would sleep during the day, pitching about the carriage, for the roads were very rough, to my very great annoyance. But during the night his anxiety kept him awake through fear, altho we had a guard of from 12 to 24 mounted horsmen each night, from sunset to sunrise, preceeding & following.

As a demonstration that this precaution was necessary, on the 2d morning after leaving Brest, just before the guard left us, we witnessed a scene that filled us with horror—the remains of a Coreir laying in the road, the master, the Postilion & 5 horses dead, laying & mangled & the mail mutilateed & scatered in all directions. We were informed, afterwards, that the Coureir was without a guard the evening previous. There had been an alarm in the visinity that had called out all their fources to suppress. Consequently, there was none to supply the last stage, & it was death, by law, for national despatches to stop. Therefore, the Master proceeded without a guard, and met the fate as discribed.

The next night, at about sun-setting, we came to a stage-stop where we expected to receive our guard, & there was none for us. However, the next stage was only five miles, & not considered very dangerous. We therefore proceeded forward, altho not without great anxiety & much preparation of our fire arms in case of an attack.

In the very neat village of Alancon, in Normandy, I had the first & only word of English spoken to me during the journey. We stopped to exchange horses & mail when the *Maitre, as usual,* was called to an account for having a passenger, & a foreigner too, in the Coureir. While he was making his justification, shewing pasports &c, a man in a tattered uniform came up to the door of the Carraige & reaching out his hand, said in quite good English: for the love of God, my dear Sir, do permit me to shake hands with one who comes from that country where the great and beloved Washington resides! He only had time to say that he had gone to America with La Fayettee and had the honour of serving under the *best man God ever made,* even the great Washington.

CHAPTER

3

I MEET
CITIZEN ROBERSPEIRE

Nothing interesting took place untill we reached Paris. It was at 4 o'clock of a beautyfull June morning when the Carriage stopped before the gate of Hotel de Boston & the bell was rung. It had been just 74 hours from the gates of Brest, during which time I had not lost myself in sleep, taken anything warm upon my stomack, nor used water upon either hands or face.

Thus covered with dust & exhausted with fategue, I was received by the Porter, conveyed to a chamber, & provided with washing apparatus. I soon freed myself from dust, applied clean linnen, and enscons'd myself in an excellent Bed, saying to myself: *soul, take thine ease in* sleep.

Maximilien François Marie Isidore de Robespierre
(6 May 1758 – 28 July 1794).
One of the best-known and most
influential figures of the French Revolution.

But it appeared that sleep had departed from me.
I laid untill the clock struck 10 without being able
to obtain a doze, & then rose. I attended to my
business thro the day and retired to Bed again
at 9 o'clock, heard the clock strike 12, and knew

nothing after untill 11'clock the next day, when I awoke feeling like myself again. (I slept soundly the next night also, 9 hours without awakening.)

After essertaining where to apply, my first object of attention was to search for my Accounts sent on from Brest. The result was that they denied, at all the offices, ever having received them or heard of such a Brig as the *Jane*, nor of her comander, Capt. Cobb.

Well, as I before observed, I prepared for this event before I left Brest by procuring a copy of my Accounts &c &c. Accordingly I laid an official set before them, thus introducing the *Jane, &* her commander. I was told to call the next day, & they would let me know when my Bills wou'd be ready. I therefore was obliged to exercise patiance & wait.

But when I called the next day, my papers were not to be found in the office. No one had put them away, no one could tell anything about them and finally, after a long French jabber, it was concluded that they must have been left upon the counter, brushed off, & burned, along with other lose papers.

This was too much for my already perplexed and agitated mind. I knew of no way but to write back to Brest for another set & these, probably, would meet the same fate as the two preseeding ones had. I was now fully conveinced that the whole was designed for the purpose of procrastination & putting off pay day as long as possible. It was a severe trial for me, in my inexperiened state.

I consulted with our consul & with our Minister at the court of France, but the only satisfaction was: git another set of papers & we will guard against another loss. While sitting with writing meterials before me in my chamber, in the act of writing for another set of papers, a French gentleman who occopied the next room & who spoke good English, passed my door.

I asked him in, & related to him my grievances. After he had thought for a few moments, he advised me to endevour to obtain an interveiw with Roberspeire, & make known to him my grievances, assuring me that he was partial to Americans & had no doubt but he would give me such advice as would be servicable to me.

I asked: "But will he, the leader of this nation, condesend to listen to a private individual & interpose in a merely comercial transaction?"

"Yes, if the business is managed right, I am confident he will."

"But how shall I obtain an interview?"

"Simply by writing him a billet yourself, in the republican stile, an American citizen, to citizen Roberspeire, & send it by a servant of the Hotel, requesting an interview about a business mattr."

After duly considering upon the subject, I wrote the following, & sent it by servant:

An American citizen, captured by a French frigate on the high seas, requests a personal interview, to lay his greivances before citizen Roberspeire.

Very Respectfully
E. Cobb

In about an hour, I received the following note in his own handwriting:

I will grant Citizen Cobb an interveiw tomorrow at 10 A. M.

Roberspiere

This gave a spring to my feelings and banished that depression which had held me in chains for some days previous. I was puntual to the time, sent my name up, & was admitted into the presence of the great man.

He pointed me to a seat without speaking. There was one man only in the Hall, an interpreter who told me that Citizen Roberspeire wished me to commince my relation from the time of my capture, and to tell the whole up to this time. I accordingly proceeded and thru the interpreter related my Capture & treatment up to that time.

Upon my closing, with a waive of Roberspeires hand, the interpreter left the hall, and he, R—e, began conversing with me in very good English, questioning me upon some perticcular points of the former conversation but more perticurly about the loss of my papers since I arrived in Paris.

Finally, he told me to call at an office in Rue St. Honorie, called the office of the 2d department, & *demand* my papers. I told him, that I had been there repeatedly, & that I was forbid to enter the office again.

Upon my telling him that, he exclaimed: *Sacra coquina!* Go, said he, to that office & tell citizen F. T. that you came from R—e, and if he does not produce your papers & finish your business *immediately* he will hear from me again in a way not so pleasing to him. At the same time he said he regreted that *his name* should be made use of in a mercantile transaction, but that my case absolutely demanded it.

I tendered my greatfull thanks for his services & left him after receiving his injunctions to call & let him know how I succeeded. I went direct to the aforesd office and by the previledge of making use of Roberspeirs name I was kindly received, an apology made for former abuses, and my business compleated the next day.

But as my exchanges were drawn payable sixty days after date, & the tribunal had decreed demurrage* &c until I had received my bills, I refused to receive them in Paris, as my pay wou'd then stop, but insisted on their being sent to the agent in Brest agreeable to contract. My object was not to receive them untill 12 or 15 days before they were due. Consequently, at no expense to myself, I remained in Paris about 3 weeks after my bills were sent to Brest. During that time the great man who had so assentially befreinded me was beheaded by the Galliotine.

This event very meterially changed the aspect of affairs in France; my exchanges, which before I could have readily sold at par value, now would not bring 50 cents. on the dollar. This induced me to go on to Hamburg with them myself and know the result.

---

*Demurrage "originated in 'vessel chartering' (notably voyage chartering) and refers to the period when the charterer remains in possession of the vessel after the period normally allowed to load and unload cargo." (Wikipedia). This means that the French were willing to pay Elijah from the time his vessel was taken until the time he received his bills—which he puts off so he'll receive remuneration as he junkets around France.

Having a desire to see more of the country & could travell at the expence of the nation, and having time before my bills wou'd come due, I took my seat in the accommodation stage for Burdeaux, visited that City, tarried 5 days, again started off and visited Nantes, Lorient & other various pleasant towns in La Vendee, arriving at Brest 20 days before my bills were due.

The agent of Merine expressed a little disapprobation at my not calling before for my Bills, having had them about 20 days, but I setled with him quite amicably and found a small vessel bound direct for Hamburg. In her, I secured a passage & embarked 3 days after.

We had a long passage, but I arrived the next day after my bills became due. And here I will relate one of those casual events which frequently take place to the benifit of man. The vessell in which I took passage stopped at Gluxstad, a town on the river Elbe about 30 miles below Hamburg. The Captain & myself went on shore & engaged a carraige to take us up to the City. But night overtaking us before we reached it, the gates were shut & we could not enter (the gates were always shut at sunsetting, & upon no occasion were opened untill sunrise).

Consequently, we turned back about a mile to the Danish city of Altony, where we put up for the night at a famous Hotel. There I found a number of american ship Masters & merchants. At the supper table, various questions were asked me, by which they learned that I was from France, that I came as a passenger. I discovered that curiosity was *wide awake* to know my business. I, however, thought it proper to keep that to myself, having fears relative to my Bills.

After riseing from the supper table, a gentleman came to me & asked me into his room. Being seated, he introduced himself as follows:

"I am, Sir, an american, from New York, my name is Loyle. I noticed the curiosity of our country-men at the supper table, to know your business & Sir, I was pleased to notice your prudent reservation upon the subject. I do not ask you, but con-jecture what it is, and if it is as I think, I can be of service to you by way of advice. My conjecture is that you have French government Bills on their agent in Hamburg. If so, I advise you to let no man know it, but go & present your demands in person. Otherwise they will be protested, for their agent, Dechapeaurouge, has already been prosecuted for paying French claims. I think, therefore, if you convince him that no one but yourself is privy to the transaction, that he may pay them."

I tended to Mr. Loyle my thanks for his information & left him. The next morning I entered the city and by enquiry soon found the office of the said agent & presented my Bill. He cast his eye upon it without speaking, then gave me a very scrutenizing look & said:

"How came you in possession of this draft?"

"I received, Sir, from M.V. la Fontaine, Minister of Marine at Brest."

"Did you receive it in person, or thro other hands?"

"I received it myself."

"Has it been in your possession ever since?"

"It has."

"Who are your freinds in this city?"

"I have none, nor even a corispondent, nor ever was in the city before, &, Sir, your office is the first & only building I ever entered in Hamburg."

"Where did you lodge last night?"

I now told him that I came as a passenger from Brest, that the vessell stopped at Gluxstaad, that I landed & hired a carriage to bring me to Hamburg, that we were too late to enter the city last night, that the driver landed me in Altona, at Lants's Hotel, where I lodged & Breakfasted this morn, that I came alone into the city & by enquiry had found his office.

He then observed, it is an unusual mode of negociating bills. It is generally done thru some resident merchant, especially by a stranger, like yourself. I told him that in so simple a transaction as that of presenting a draft for acceptance, I felt myself competant to the task, and thereby save paying a commission.

Well, said he, you have acted discreetly, took a pen & wrote *accepted* across the face of the Bill. He then said: your money is ready for you, but this draft must not go out of my hands again, for if it does, it never will be paid by me.

This embarrassed me extremely. What could I do with 40,000 crowns in silver in my situation, an entire stranger in a strange City? After a moments reflection, I said to him:

"Will you, Sir, give me your due bill & allow me to receipt the draft?"

"Certainly," said he, "I will."

Accordingly, it was done. This, I knew, was exchanging the obligation of a great & powerfull nation for that of a private individual, but I thought that circomstances justified the Act. I then asked him if he would name to me a house of entertainment frequented by Americans, & he ordered a servant to conduct me to Lilbons Hotel.

And thus closed the important interveiw with De Chapeaurouge, & I found his *due Bill,* as good as Cash. Thus, how fortunate the circomstance of my interveiw with Mr. Loyle. But for his kind information & advice I shou'd, no doubt, have put my draft into the hands of the American Consul for collection; the consequence would have been, a protest and another tour to France to seek redress. And all this saved by the Gates being shut before I reached them.

How often, my dear Grand Children, do we repine and murmer, when disappointment, affliction, and trouble come upon us, & even distrust the goodness of our Heavenly Father, when we, very frequently, afterwards realize that it was for our good.

It was somewhat so with me. I felt very much put out at the gates being shut, & chided the driver for his dilatoryness, when he knew the city gates closed at sun-sett—but this very circomstance was the means of freeing my mind from a burden which had weighed it down for months. It was the means of a happy, and prosperous termination of my labourous voyage, for nothing now remained to be done but to remitt the funds to T. Dickerson & Sons, London, & to take passage for Boston myself, & give an account of my stewardship to my employers. And all this I could do with bouyant sperits, having made them an excellent voyage.

I was not long in closing my business in Hamburg, & took passage for Boston in the ship *Warren*, Capt. Hodgkins, where we safely arrived after a passage of 54 days. My arrival gave great relief to my owners for, from the accounts they had from France, they doubted the validity of my Bills on Hamburg, & expected I wou'd have to return to France. The fortunate close of this tedious voyage, and my return, being the first instance of the kind under the state of things in France at the time, produced no small excitement among the merchants of Boston who had property in France, and application was continually made to me for all the whys & wherefores relative to the fortunate result of my business. The consequence was: it added greatly to my fame as a ship master.

CHAPTER

ANOTHER VOYAGE
TO FRANCE

Another voyage was immediately planned by my owners for France, & I was only allowed a very few days to visit my family. Although our first child (now Aunt Sampson) was but 24 hours old when I left home, when I return'd she could say, my *par.* But short, indeed, was the time alloted me for injoying the objects of my affection, for I must leave them and persue the road marked out for obtaining that subsistance for myself & family which nature required and reason dictated.

After staying at home 4 days only, I returned to Boston, fitted out my vessel, & sailed for Alexandria & there purchased a cargo of Flour & sail'd for

France. On my arrival in Harvre de grace, I found that the government purchased all the flour that came to market. Consequently, I sold my cargo to the governments agent, at 20 crowns pr bbl, under a promis that I sho'd have my pay in 40 days after delivery.

But I found, to my sorrow, that no confidence could be placed in their pledges, & that I was again subjected to a tedious altercation with the agent & his government. After dancing attendance upon them about 2 1/2 months (my vessell, at the same time, laying Idle & at a great expence) I again concluded to send her home under charge of the mate, & stay myself, & fight it out. Accordingly, I dispatchd the Brig & went on to Paris, prepared for the seige & expecting a long one.

In about two months more I received about one third of my demand in Ingots of silver, & made a trip over to London, & deposited this amount with Bird, Savage, & Bird, subject to my owners order. I then returned to France, and renewed my claim for the remainder.

And after about three months more of atten-dance upon the government of France, I received the ballance due me—about 40,000 Crowns. Here, probably, you will conclude that my anxiety terminated. But, on the conterary, it was, if posible, increased. I had attained the object of several months of contention with the french government. I had on hand a fine voyage for my employers, but the great difficulty now was how I should git the property out of France.

There was a special law against exporting *specie* from the country. Exchanges were not to be obtained in which my confidence could be placed; my vessell was gone, so that investing in goods was out of the question.

I had brought publickly the 40,000 crowns to my sleeping chamber at noon-day. Thus situated, you may judge whether my mind could be at ease! However, having taken the necessary precaution-ary measures against robery or theft, I went to work, & purchasd all the *foreign Gold* I could find in order to git the value into a smaller bulk for the purpose of smuggling it out of France.

After about two months with the help of my agents in Paris & Roen & my own in Harvre de grace, I succeeded in converting my 40,000 crowns into less than 3000 peices of gold, prinsapally, Spanish doubloons. This had been done in as secret a manner as posible.

I then went to a village about 3 miles away & ordered 2 leather belts made of a sufficient size to hold 8 or 9 hundred peices, and after puting each peice into a wrapper of silk paper, I sowed my belts & stiched them in such a manner that there could be no motion of the pieces. The two belts contained 1700 pieces. The remainder I made up into wads of about 50 peices each, enveloped in paper & cloth.

I then engaged my passage for Boston in the ship *Caroline*, Capt Cutter, and after two or three days the ship hauled out of the basin and stopped opposite the custom house, within Six rods of my Lodgings. Having free access to the ship at all times, I soon decided how to dispose of the money not contained in the two belts. In a short time it was safely & secretly stowed away on board the ship.

On the morning of the day on which the ship was to sail, I pursuaded the ships Steward (with the promise of a guinea) to put one of the Belts round his waist & wear it untill we were clear from the peir head. The other belt I secured to my own person, and thus curcomstanced I had to submitt to the scearch by 8 french officers, at the head of whom was an old experienced Searcher who strongly suspected that there was money on board. But not withstanding all, I got off clear with my money, and after a passage of 35 days I had the satisfaction of delivering it to my owners in Boston.

CHAPTER

This is the house that Elijah built in 1799, still standing on the Lower Road in Brewster, Massachusetts.

ADVENCHURES IN NORTH EUROPE

❖❖✖○✖○✖○✖❖❖

On my return home, I found that my pert-ner in lifes voyage had run me in debt for a cape Cod farm. As the place was distitute of a suitable building for the accommodation of our little family, it was thought advisable to proceed to errect one. I consequently felt myself under the necesity of declining business in the sea-faring line, and attend to that of a more domestic nature for a while.

I remained at home from August 1798 untill Sept 1799. As the events of this year are something remarkable, I will name a few of them. This year, 1799, the beloved Washington, the Father of our

Country, died. This year, our first son was born. This year I took possession of the farm, built my house, and the family moved into it on new years day 1800.

In October, 1799, I took charge of the Brig Mary, went to Savannah, in Georgia, from ther to Lisbon, from thence to London, to Rotterdam, Copenhagen, St. Petersburg, and back to Boston & performed the voyage in 8 months & 4 days.

After remaining at home a short time, I received a letter offering me the charge of a new ship called the *Monsoon*. I accordingly repaired to Boston & took charge of her. She was owned by the Messrs Hayden & Baxter, Mr. Joshua Hall, & Jacob Tidd. They put on board a valuable Cargo, & ordered me to find a Market for it in some part of the north of Europe. But as I had in the cargo a quantity of American Rum, they recomended that I shou'd touch on Ireland, upon the supposition that if I cou'd obtain permission to land it that it would command a high price.

I accordingly made my way for Cork, and after a passage of 26 days arrivd at the Cove of Cork.

This was meerly a harbour & a village of a few thousand inhabitants. I landed & proceeded to the City, which was about 12 miles above and called upon the House of Jno. & Isaac Carrel & Co. to whoom I had a letter of introduction. They received me very politely, but doubted my obtaining permission to land the rum even if I was willing to pay foreign duty. They, however, went with me to the custom house to consult with the collector who, I found, was in favour of landing it but dare not give permission without consulting his superiors in the office. He said he wou'd attend to it & have an answer in a few days.

I returned on board my ship in the evening & found her in possession of 3 custom house officers, siezed, ship and cargo, with the Kings seal upon her hatches. When I enquired the cause, I found it was for having on board sperits not of the growth & manufactory of the British plantations.

I called upon the deputy collector who had ordered the Seizure of the ship. He appeared so pleasant upon the subject that I felt quite a releif. I consequntly return'd to the city & called again upon the Collector.

He told me I would have to apply *in person* to the Admirllty of Dublin relative to the Seizure of the ship, & he at the same time wou'd write them relative to landing the sperits. I consequntly post'd off for the City of Dublin, a journey of about 200 miles, & arrived there without accident. I was much amused in traveling thro the hart of Ireland and observing the Irish people, in their symplicity of manners and appearance, almost in a state of nature.

I called upon the board of Admirallity and after a lengthy investigation in which I employed council, it was found that the ship & cargo was forfeited to the crown, and was ordered fourthwith to be advertisd & sold at publick Auction. It was, however, intimated to me (in private) that this was a sham, & that I wou'd have liberty to buy ship & Cargo at my own price.

And so it proved, for when I returned to Cork I found the ship advertised, to be sold in 3 days. I appeard at the time & place. The ship & cargo, with all appertunances, were set up together, to be sold for Cash down. Some one freindly to me bid 2/6. I then bid 5s/ and the whole was struck off to me—and thus I was again in possession of ship and Cargo.

Finding no prospect of obtaining permission to land the rum, I concluded to proceed elswhere for a Market for my Cargo, and was advised to try the Island of Geurnsey. Therefore I applied to the custom House to clear the ship, which was readily complied with. The collector observed to me when about taking leave: "Capt. Cobb, I must confess, I think your usage has been something rough here. I shou'd not blame you if you was to help yourself a little, in the way of smuggling."

"No Sir," said I, "for wou'd you not be one of the first to make a prize of me?"

"Oh," said he, "I shou'd have to do my duty."

"Well Sir," said I, "when you *Catch'em* you *Hab'em.*"

"God blesse you," said he, & thus we parted.

The next morn I sail'd; matters were, however, so arrainged that between the cove of Cork & the

Scilly Islands, I hove overboard Eight hogheads of N. E. rum, and a pilot boat sheer'd along side, and hove on board a small bag, which I found contained 264 English guineas. I saw them pick up & hoist on board the 8 hhds of rum, and *I was satisfied.*

I then proceeded for my Port of distination, Geurnsey, an Island in the channel of England, which had always been a free port & a resort for Smugglars. I anchord in the roads about sun's setting & having a letter of introduction from a friend in Cork to a merchant here, I took my boat & went ashore, altho the hour was an improper one, *the dusk of Eve.*

Being an entire stranger, I had to make enquiries; finally, in about an hour, I found the Gent to whom the letter was addressed. He recd. me with politeness and read the letter. I apologised for calling upon him at so unseasonable an hour. He promptly replied, it is fortunate for you, that you have thus done. I am now, Sir, compelled to act a part which not only appears *uncivil,* but almost to an insult. Viz, that you return immediately on board your ship and leave this port.

He then, in a few words, told me that the British parlement had recently passed revenue laws that affected that Island; & that two English cutters had that day arrived to inforce the laws, & that I shou'd certainly have trouble with my cargo if I was not off before sun rise the next morning.

I accordingly bid the gentleman good bye, repaird to my boat, which was waiting for me at the wharf, went on board the ship & immediately got underway. At sun rise, the next morn, I was out of sight of the Island of Geurnsay up channell, on my way for the City of Hamburg.

Thus ended my deficulties of that voyage. I arrived safe in Hamburg, found a good Market for my cargo, loaded my ship, & returned to Boston, having made a good voyage to all concern'd.

My employers were so well pleased with the trade I had opened in Hamburg that they planned another voyage immediately, and thot they cou'd hardly afford me time to visit my family at the cape. However, by promis's of a short stay, I came to Brewster; saw my family, and returned to Boston to fit out the ship for another Voyage.

My owners concluded that it wou'd be for the Interest of the Voyage, that on my arrival in H—g I should land my Cargo, load the ship with a return cargo, & send her home by my Mate. I was to remain in Hamburg myself thro the Winter, to sell the cargo just landed and prepare another for the ship on her return to me in the spring.

Under the foregoing arrangement, I saild for Hamburg a 2d time; arrived their after a common passage, landed my Cargo, loaded the ship with Russia & Germain goods, and sent her for Boston under the command of my mate, David Nickerson. She sailed the last of September, and by the middle of Novr we were compleatly bound in fetters of *Frost.* In that high Lattitude we had only about 7 hours day light in 24, but there was no lack of *amusements,* to please the eye, taste, or mind.

I injoyed myself very well untill the last of Decembr when I received a letter which came overland by way of Holland, from one of my employers. In it was stated in a Postcrip: *Your wife has been very Sick, but, I beleive, she is better.* This unwellcome intiligence, the uncouth manner in which it was conveyed to me, and the great uncertainty of hearing anything more untill my ship returned to me, put my mind into a perplexing state of anxiety, which bid defiance to all in joyment of life.

Within a few days, as I entered the coffee room of the Hotel in the morning, the servant said to me: there is an american Newspaper which arrived last evening, by way of London. I took up the paper, and the first thing that attracted my notice was my *Brothers death*.

Thus the mind, already bowed down with anxiety, was obliged to receive this *heartrending* addition to its already overcharged burden. In addition to my afflixtions then, I was attactd with the *brain* fever, with such severity that for 8 days was unconcious of either pleasure, or pain.

I was, finally, permitted to recover, with the loss only of my full head of black hair. I got over that deficuty *pritty* well by substituting a Wig, and have been obliged to wear one ever since to keep my head warm.

But our heavenly Father lays no more upon his children than He knows they can bear. Notwithstanding all, I was supported thro the winter. My business, by the help of merchants, Brokers &c, went on well, and when the ship arrived, about the 20th of May, I was ready & prepared for her, and the news she brot. me from my family was a cordial to my lasserated feelings.

As soon as the Cargo which the ship brot out cou'd be sold, the arrangements made during the winter were such that we were soon ready for returning to Boston. I reach'd home in Augst, having been absent somthing over 14 months and found Mrs C. very feeble, but convallessent.

CHAPTER

MORE AVENCHURES IN EUROPE

I made one more voyage to Hamburg in the Monsoon. When I return'd she was sold, which gave me an oppertunity of spending a few weeks at home with my beloved family. But it was not long before I received a letter from Mr. J. Tidd, who was one of my former owners in the Monsoon, requesting me to come to Boston fourthwith, as there was a new Brig for sale which he had an idea of purchasing, and wished for my opinion &c &c. I accordingly went to Boston & the Brig *Sally & Mary* was purchased. Another Hamburg voyage was plann'd fourthwith.

Mr. Tidd put on board a valuable cargo on his own account & risk, and ordered me for

Hamburg. Accordingly I proceeded for the river Elbe. It being in the summer season, I took the more direct passage of "north about", so called, viz. between the Okney & Shetland Islands, into the North sea, at the S E part of which the river Elbe commences. Hamburg is 100 miles above.

Heretofore I had always obtained a Pilot before I reach'd the entrance of the river, but now none appeared, and I saw at anchor, in the mouth of the river, one large ship & 2 or 3 smaller vessels. It struck me at once that the Elbe was block-aded*, but I had no alternative but to proceed on & find out. I accordingly run on untill within about a mile of the largest ship, when I came to an anchor. She immediately sent her boat on board, for me & my papers.

I found the commander was a *haughty, crabbed, self willed,* Scotchman. He insisted that I knew of the blockade and that I intended a breach of it. Of course, I was a good prize, & he would send me to England.

---

*This was the so-called Fox blockade, 1806 (Fox was the British foreign minister at the time). It put 800 miles of North European coast out of bounds for trade.

Very well! I had to submitt to his superior force and I was accordingly ordere'd for Yarmouth in England. On my arrival there, my papers were sent to London, to the Kings advocate for adjudication. They were returnd in 6 days, & I was pronounced clear, to proceed to any port that was not blockaded. I put to sea the next morning.

As I cou'd not go to Hamburg, I concluded that Copenhagen would be the next *best* market for my Cargo. I accordingly steered my course for that port. On my arrival there, I was advised by a freindly Danish Merchant to proceed to *Lubec*, one of the *Hans Towns* of Germany, about 100 miles South of Copenhagen, (on the great Belt, so called). From this place an inland canal communicated with Hamburg and my Cargo could be readily sent in defiance of the Blockade. As my Cargo was perticularly selected for the Hamburg Market, this was a very important object with me.

I consequently proceeded for Lubec where I arrived in about 48 hours. I was told that I displayed the first American flag ever wafted over their City! On approaching the Town, an entire stranger, I recolected that on my last voyage to

Hamburg a Mr. Smidth of the Firm of Smidth & Plefsing, of Lubec, had made a shipment of 100 peices of Duck by me, which I had sold & made returns to them.

I was now glad to enquire them out and avail myself of their services in selling my cargo & purchaseing another on my return &c &c. I very readily found them and received from them all those kind attentions to me and my business so greatfull to a Stranger. A great part of my cargo went thro the canal to Hamburg, and also much of my return cargo came back the same way. I found a good Market, got quick dispatch, and returned to Boston with an excellent voyage.

After discharging my cargo in Boston, I visited my dear family at the cape, where I found an additional pledge of affection, in a little black-eye'd daughter, which we call'd Mary P, then 69 days old. It being in the night, & no light in the house, I hawl'd her out of Bed, and held her up to the window to look at her by moonlight.

I was permitted to remain but a short time in the enjoyment of the family circle before I receiv'd a letter saying that another voyage was planned, & I must come forward. Accordingly, I went on to Boston, & found they had began loading the Brig, for a voyage to Malaga.

The loading was soon compleated and necessary preperations made. I saild for the Medeterenaen & arrived at Malaga November 12th, 1807. On my arrival, I was informed that the *celebrated British orders in council* had gone into fource *there* the day before I arrived. Those orders forbid american vessells to take a return cargo from any port in Europe, under the penalty of being a prize in any English port.*

In consequence of this, we knew that *wines* & *fruit* wou'd rapidly advance in price in America, which made a return cargo very desirable. The *American Consul,* with whom I advised, thought if I got quick dispatch there wou'd be but little risk

---

*The Orders forbade French trade with the United Kingdom, its allies, or neutrals, and instructed the Royal Navy to blockade French and allied ports. When Cobb relates that he took on a cargo of wine and fruit, it is difficult to understand how he would be allowed to do so, since Spain was a satellite state of the Napoleonic Empire. Apparently the English were enforcing the blockade only at Gibralter so that on-loading cargo at Malaga presented no immediate problem.

in my taking a return cargo and that he wou'd obligate himself to dispatch me in 10 days with a full cargo of wine and fruit. I finally concluded to take the risk.

Accordingly I proceeded to discharge my cargo & receive on board wine & fruit in return, & in 8 days was ready to sail. In order to succeed in escaping an investigation & probably a capture by the English, I thot to wait for a strong easterly wind, and to improve the night, to make a run through the *Gut of Gibralter,* where lay the greatest danger of capture or detention. I accordingly awaited the first Easterly wind & left Melaga, calculating to reach the rock of Gibralter about Dark the same Eve, which I did.

But unfortunally, as I approach'd the wind died away, and by time I had pass'd, it was nearly calm. Knowing that if it remained so thro the night, that daylight would expose me to the Fort & their cruizers, and I should surely be exposed to examination & detention. I thought it advisable to proceed to Anchorage with what wind I had, and I immediately hawled into the Bay, steering for the neutrial ground. But the wind being ahead,

I had to make a tack under the Spanish shore, & while standing over for the rock, was boarded by the boat of an English Frigate, commanded by a mid-shipman who took charge of me, under pretence that I was bound into Algaziras.

After we had come to anchor, although it was 12 o'clock at night, he insisted upon taking me on board the Frigate with my papers. Well, I was conducted on board & brought before an officer who questioned me. I told him the truth: that I was from Malaga, bound to Boston, that I had come in there to evail myself of a clearence from a British port & a convoy thro the gut.

"Well," said he, "a convoy will sail, the day after tomorrow." He ordered the officer to carry me on board my vessell again immediately. I went on shore the next morn & calld upon the American consel, to whom I made known my true situation. He told me he thought there was but little chance for me, as I was compleatly under the *Orders in Council.*

I left the consul, & in the street fell in with an old acquaintance. To him I told my grievance. He advised me: as a last resort, & as my situation was

not generally known, to endevour to effect a cler-
ance by bribery, & he gave other advice & information upon that subject. I accordingly went on
board, got my papers, put a couple of ounces of
spanish gold into my pocket & went on shore &
directly to the office on the Quay. I found only
the *Principall* in the office.

I told him I commanded an American vessell from
Malaga, bound to Boston, and had put in there to
obtain a clearance & a convoy thro the Gut.

"Well," said he, "as you say you have a cargo on
board, there are some serious questions to ask,
previous to your obtaining a clearance."

"I know, I know Sir, but do not be too particular.
Give me a clearance." At the same time I laid on
the counter before him, *two ounce peices of gold.*

"Well," said he, "if I give you a clearance, you
have another office to git signed at."

"Well," said I, "if you will give it, there will be
less deficulty."

As I spoke a gentleman came into the office, to whom the first observed:

"This Captain was just going up to your office with his clearance. Will you be so kind as to save him the trouble by signing it here?"

"Oh yes," said he cheerfully.

Accordinly, in a few minuits my clearance was compleated, the fees of both offices paid, & I was in the street, making a streight wake towards the American consul. When I entered his office, he, with a long face said:

"I am glad to see you, but greatly regret your situation." I took my clearance from my pocket & held it before his *eyes*.

"*Good God,*" said he, "how did you git that?"

Said I, "ask me no questions & I will tell you no lies."

The Signal Gun was fired at sun-rise the next morn for the convoy to weigh, & I was one of the first to move, for I was full of fear that some incident might *yet* subject me to the *fatal* investigation, and I was therefore desirous to git out of their reach. A large English merchant ship showing a teir of guns, streched over for the Barbary coast & I followed her under easy *sail. Our convoy,* a gun Brig, was not then underway and in watching for her, I discovered a boat after us, full of men, rowing & sailing.

I immediately felt they were *after me.* I ordered sail immediately put on, & in a very short time, the boat *gave up* & put back for Gibralter. Then I was anxious fearing the convoy might have orders to bring me back, but I heard nothing more, parted from the convoy off cape Trafelgar.

(In regard to the boat that was after me—sometime after I arrived home, I fell in with a Capt Mills, whom I left at Malaga in a Brig belonging to Boston. Persueing the same plan as I had done, he saild from Malaga the day after me, was taken into Gibrater the night before I left. Seeing me underweigh, without reflection, he observed: there is Cobb, why is he allowed to go? The boat was immediately dispatch'd after me, but by my vigilence in making sail in good season, & being favored with a good stiff breeze I was enable'd to keep clear of them.)

CHAPTER

THE EMBARGO

Ballasted with stones, I returned to Norfolk in Virginia, where I found letters from my Owners with orders to go up to Alexandria & load.*

While this process was in opperation, a most violent *storm* came on, & as I had discharg'd most

---

*The preceding chapter sees Cobb leaving Gibralter with a contraband load of fruit and wine in mid-November, 1807. Now he describes returning with stone ballast. There would not have been sufficient time for more than the voyage home, between mid-November (after taking 8 days to procure and load cargo) and December 20, when he arrived in Alexandria. The reader will have to live with this discrepancy, remembering that Cobb was quite elderly by the time he got this far in his Recollections.

of the crew, I was on board assisting in secureing the ship to the Wharf when Mr. Fisk, a Merchant with whom I advised, came down the wharf & told me that he had just received a *dispatch* from Mr. Randolph, in Congress, saying to him: *what you do must be done quickly* for the embargo will be upon you, on Sunday at 10 A.M.

It was now Fryday P.M., in the middle of a violent storm.

"Well," said Mr. F, "what can we do, Cobb?"

"Why," said I, "if we can hold the ship to the wharf while it blows so hard, I shall be glad. And we can see where we can git the cargo, & if it is fair to morrow much may be done."

In fact much must be accomplish'd in order to effect our object viz. *to cheat the Embargo.* We had about 100 Tons of stone Ballast on board which must be landed, upward of 3000 bbls of Flour to take in and stow away, provisions, wood & water to take on board, a crew to ship, and clearance at the custom House, and git the ship to sea before the Embargo would be in force. All this must

be done between Saturday morn at day light &
sunday morn at 10 o'clock.

We found, upon enquiry, that we cou'd have our
supply of Flour from a block of stores directly
along side of the Ship, & by giving 3/8th of a
dollar extra, we had liberty, if stopped by the
embargo, to return it.

Saturday morning was fine weather. I had given
instructions to the mates to discharge ballast at
the main hatchway & to receive the Flour forward and abaft (the ship having three hatch-
ways), with two gangs of Stevidores in the hold.
About Sunrise, I went up to *lazy corner*, so call'd,
& pressed every Negro into my service that
came there & sent them on board the ship, untill
I thought there were as many in the hold as could
work.

I then visited the Sailors boarding houses, where
I shipped my crew, paid the advance to their
landlords, & obtained their agreement to see
each sailor on board at sun-rise the next morning. It had now got to be about 12 o'clock & the
ship must be cleared at the Custom house at, or

before, 1:00. I accordingly prepared a Manifest & went to the Custom house to clear the Ship.

Mr. Taylor, the collector, knowing my situation, *said:*

"Why Cobb, what is the use of clearing the ship? You cannot git away. The embargo will be here at 10 tomorrow morning, & even if you get down river, I shall have boats out that will stop you before you can git 3 leagues to sea."

Said I, "Mr. Taylor, will you be so kind as to clear my Ship?"

"Oh yes," said he, "I cannot refuse untill the embargo arrives."

Accordingly the ship was cleared & I returned on board & found all things going on well. Finally— to shorten the Story—at 9 that evning, we had on board 3050 Barrels of Flour, our long boat on board in the chocks, water, wood, & provision on board & stowed, a pilot engaged, & all in readi- ness for Sea.

The tide wou'd not serve until 8 o'clock on sunday morn, and at 10 the embargo was expected. Well, the morn arrived, the sailors were brot on board by their Landlords, the pilot came on, & at 8 o'clock we started with a fair wind, down a crooked nerrow river.

But the wind dying, our progress was Slow, & when we entered Hampton roads, it had got to be after 11 o'clock and nearly calm. Feeling anxious, I kept a sharp look out astern, & at 12 I saw with my glass a boat comeing down under the full opperation of sails & oars.

"Well," said I to the mate, "I fear we are gone."

But very soon I saw the appearance of a fresh breeze coming off from the South shore. I saw that the approaching boat had already taken it. I then ordered all the light sails set, ready to receive the breeze. When it reached us, the boat was so near that with my glass I could trace the features of the men on her. But in 10 munutes the boat give up the chace & turn'd back, and I went to sea without further molestation.

By the pilot I wrote my Owners, informing them of my running away from the Embargo, & then proceeded on for Cadiz, carrying there the first news of Mr. Jefferson's folly. Flour was selling, on my arrival, at $16.00 but in consequence of the Embargo & the war then rageing in that vicinity, the flour holders had a meeting, & agreed to raise the price to $20.00. Finally, altho I waited some time, I obtained that price for my Cargo.*

*The Embargo lasted better than a year. It was repealed in March 1809, allowing ships to sail but forbidding them to trade with England or France. The time frame is uncertain in the captain's memoir, but it seems probable that Cobb made several more voyages, most likely to Spain. The narrative, then, starts again in 1812.

CHAPTER

8

WAR OF
1812

Several years later, I was in Cadiz when I recd. a letter by a vessell under Sweedish colours, adviseing me to bring home money, providing there was liberty to export it. Finding, upon enquiry, that this was the case, I immediately took out a license from the custom house to export $72,000, having funds here from the last voyage.

But before I got ready to sail I heard of the repeal of the orders in Council, & also, of the *Milan & Berlin* decrees.* Beleiving this would have a

---

*The repeal of British Orders in Council was England's response to American outage at the ongoing impressment of U.S. sailors. However, America had declared war two days before the Orders were rescinded, and it took a month for this information to reach Europe. No one in Cadiz yet knew that the war had already begun.

favourable effect to America in our Exchanges, & finding I cou'd buy British government Bills at a great discount, I decided to give up my Licinse & remitt my money to England.

(I mention this circomstance to shew how fortunate it was, as I was captured on my way home. If the Money had been on board, we shou'd have lost it.)

The day before I sailed I dine'd in a large party at the american consul, & it being mention'd that I was to sail the next day, I was congratulated by a British officer upon the safety of our Flagg. Well, I thot the same, when at the same time, the War between England & America was then rageing and I knew not of it.

I sail'd from Cadiz, the 5th. day of July 1812 bound for Boston, & I never felt myself safer on account of enemies on the high seas. I had just entered upon the eastern edge of the Grand Bank at day light of the morn of the 17th. I went on deck; we had a light breeze of wind from the north, with all sails sett that would draw. In casting my eye to windward, I saw a sail, to appearance bearing down directly for us.

Not having bespoken any vessel yet, I told the mate to back the main yard & I would speak her. We accordingly did & at sunrise I ordered the Insign hoisted at the Mizen peak. No sooner were our colours up than his went up along with the smoke of a gun. I saw that she was a Schooner under English colours & that she was armed.

But I was not alarmed. I continud to lay by & she run down acrosst my stern with the usual hail of: where from? where bound? How long out? &c &c

He concluded from my replys that I did not know that war existed. He said to me, very mildly, I will thank you to continue laying by, & I will send my boat for you. Seeing she was a cutter Schooner with 10 brass Guns, I, of course, acquiesed & her boat came along side with two petty officers, rowed by *only* two men.

One of the officers requested me to go on board the cutter with my papers. Well, I invited the 2 officers below while I moved my things around and got the papers. While I was in my statroom, one of them says to me:

"Captn, what cargo did you carry to Cadiz?"

"Flour."

"You got a good price, I presume?"

"Yes," said I.

"Got cash on board, I suppose?"

"No, I remitted my money to England."

"Well," said he, "You've a fine ship here!"

"Yes, tolorble."

"What," said he, "do you think she's worth?"

This question roused my curiosity. I step'd to the door of the Stateroom, & looking the man in the face, said to him: "Have you an Idea of buying, or taking the ship?"

"Oh," said he, "Captain, you'll excuse our inquisitiveness. It was without meaning."

When I was ready, one of the officers went in the boat with me & the other remained on board the my ship. I was received on board the cutter & conducted into the Capt's cabin. He received my papers & looking them over, ask'd if I had not a Clearance from Cadiz. I told him I had, but I did not know it wou'd be required, so I had not brot it with me.

"Well," said he, "I must have it."

"If you'll send your boat back, Sir, I will go & look it up. I think it's in my writing desk."

"Well," said he, "send for your desk."

I told him I was unwilling to do that, as it contained papers of consequence to me & by accident it might be dropped overboard.

"Oh," said he, "I'll make good all damages, you *must* send for it."

Well, I wrote a line to the mate to send my Desk. It was brought into the cutter's cabin. Having my keys in my pocket, I open'd it & soon found the paper required. As the desk, standing upon the Table, was open, the officers standing around began looking at my papers. Among them was a small bundle of letters directed to the Commissary Generl of the *Quebec Station.* They open'd it & broke the seal of one of the letters. I look'd at the Capt & observ'd that this was treatment which I had not anticipated from the British flagg.

The Capt observ'd, "you must submit. We will explain ourselves bye. & bye." About this time, the word came from the decks: a *Strange sail in sight,* & the Capt, drop'd the paper & ran on deck.

I set still & wached the officers overhawling & deranging my papers in my writing desk. After a while the Capt came down below & said to me: "Captain, you have expressed some surprise at our investigation, at which I am not at all supprised, for I find you are ignorant of a fact which will justify our proceedings with you. We are *at War with America.*"

"Now, sir," said I, "I believe you are disposed to *tantalize*, for I do not beleive it."

"Well, Sir," said he, "we will not altercate upon this subject." He step'd to a desk, took out a news-paper & pointed me to the declaration of War, & danced on deck again to look at the Strange sail. The paper that he handed me was an American paper, only 12 days old. After reading the decla-ration of war, I look'd it over for other news untill the Capt came back down. He then said to me: "Well Sir, what think ye now?"

I told him I was satisfied as to war, but I shou'd like to know now, whether I was to be *hung*, or *drounded.*

He, smiling said: "Well, I beleive nither, not *by me.* I will now," said he, "explain to you the rea-sons for our conduct toward you. I am," said he, "from Halifax, bound to England with dispatches for the Govt. I cannot take you, not having men to man your ship. If I had found money on board I shou'd have taken it & put one man on board, so that it might not be call'd piricy, & let you have your chance. But as it is, you can take charge of your ship & do the best you can. The sail approaching is an American Frigate, & if I can keep out the reach of her guns, I will do so. The sooner you go back to your ship the better."

"As soon as you please," said I, & crowded some of my papers into my Desk & tied some up in a hankerchief & thus went into the boat & was set on board my own ship again. When I got on deck, the Frigate was coming down with all sail set, so near that she cou'd easyly have sent a shot over me. Altho she was flying an American Insign at her Mizinpeak, I suspected she was an English Frigate. Still, being compleatly within the reach of her guns, & my ships sails all taken in, I could only lay still & take it.

The Frigate was down in a few minuits and the boats were manned. A party came on board under the command of an officer, in an American uniform. The usual questions, of where from, where bound, how long out &c &c, were ask'd & ansered, when he thus asked: "Are you not in fear of being taken?"

"No Sir," said I, "for I think I am *already* taken."

"What?" said he. "By one of your own Frigates?"

"No," said I, "this is not an american Frigate. Nither, Sir, are *you* intitled to wear that Badge."

"Well," said he, "you are about right. This is His Britianic majistys Frigate, the *Jason*, & you are her prize. Now," said he, "what have you on board for Cargo?"

"Sand Ballast," said I.

"What did you cary to Cadiz?"

"Flour."

"Did it sell?"

"Yes, it Brought $20.00 pr Barrel."

"Oh, you've Cash on board," said he.

"No," said I, "I remitted the proceeds of my cargo

to London, & I have my thirds of exchange, to satisfy you."

"Well," said he, "you have a fine ship here. What will you give for her, in exchange for a clear passport into Boston?"

After a little reflection, I name'd $5000.00.

"Well," said he, *"give us the money."*

"O, thank you," said I. "If it was on board, you wou'd take it without asking me. I will give you a draft on London."

"No," said he, *"the cash,* or we *burn* the ship."

"Well," said I, "you'll not burn me in her, I hope."

"Oh, no, you may give orders for your men to pick up their duds, & we will carry them on board the Frigate. You will remain on board & select yourself a servant from your crew. The ship is too good to *Burn.*"

Accordingly, I selected my Nephew, E. C. Crosby,

to remain with me. My mates & crew were all carried on board the Frigate. After a while, the pinnace was sent with special orders for me to come on board the Frigate.

Well, I went on Board, was received at the Gangway by a Leutenent, & conducted into the captain's Cabin, where he, with his officers, were then sitting at the dinner table. I was place'd in a chair by the captain's side & offered a glass of wine, after which he (the capt) said to me:

"What D—d rascal put your papers in that situation?" (for they were brot to him just as I took them from the cutter, open letters &c.)

"Why, Sir," said I, "that D—d rascal, as you are pleas'd to call him, was Leutenant Jones, commanding his Majesties cutter the Alphea."

"Why," said he, "he's broke the Kings Seal. I'll have the fellow hung."

"Well Sir," said I, "you can do as you please with your own subjects."

He then said to me, "I am satisfied, on examination of your papers, that you have not money on board as a return cargo, but I shall now ask you a question which it will be in your Interest, to answer *candidly*."

"Well Sir, I shall judge better, when I hear the question!"

"Have you money on board, on your own private account?"

Without hesitation, I answer'd, "Yes."

"How much?" said he.

"About $2000."

"It is safe. We as yet respect private property when it does not exceed $3000. More than that we think is smugled. Finally," he observed, "your officers & men, now on board here, shall fare as we do."

"Well, Sir, we have abundant provisions on

board the prise. If you'l permit, I'l send some by the boat that returns with me."

"Certainly," said he, "& it shall be kept for them exclusively while they are on board this ship. I have put a prise master & crew on board your ship, & ordered her for St Johns. I shall visit that coast in 8 or 10 days, & will then deliver up your officers & crew. I will now send you on board. I have charged the prise master not to intefere with, but to conform to your regulations, &c &c."

I return'd on board, & we made sail for St Johns as ordered. I found the prise Master a very pleasant man, & all things went on pleasantly. Due to adverse winds, it was 6 days before we arrived at St. Johns in the evening.

The next morn I was taken on shore & conducted before the Port Admiral, Sir John Thomas Duckworth. After he had made enquiries relative to my voyage, capture &c &c he told me that I had the liberty of the town provided I choose to take up my residence on shore, or, I had the liberty of remaining on board the ship, but could not have axcess to both.

I finally told him that I wou'd like to remain on board the ship untill my officers & men were sent in, after which I wou'd like to come on shore.

Accordingly, I returned to the ship, where I was allowed the same use of my cabin & provisions as formally. In 4 days, my officers & crew were sent in, and we were again altogether on board the ship. As we had remaining a shoat of about 60 lb, I ordered it dressed, & a good dinner provided for all hands and myself.

The next day I took up my residence on shore, at prisiners Hall, so called, where there were about 20 Masters & supercargoes & prisinners like myself. I found that there were 27 American vessells in port, as prises. The Port Admiral had given liberty to the Supercaroes & Gentlemen passengers to leave & git home at there own expence, provided they went away altogether. He would give them protection against capture by the English.

As I had two Brothers on board my ship, Josiah & E. C. Crosby, the Idea struck me that it was *posible* I might be allowd to send the latter home with the others who were already given permission. They had already purchas'd a small vessell, & were then fitting her out. He was a meer boy, so I accordingly drafted a request to Sir John, stating in as feeling a manner as I was capable, the inconsolibility of his Parents &c &c, and waited upon the old Gentleman with it in person. He looked it over attentively, then looked up at me & said: "Yes, Yes, Mr Cobb, send him home to his parents. I wish I cou'd say the same to all of you."

I accordingly made preparations for sending the boy home. I wrote to my family by him, and also stitched 20 peices of Spanish Gold into a packet, worth about $380. He put it into his neck hankerchief & there wore it, night & day, untill he got home took it from his neck & gave it to his Aunt.

Six days after the vessell had saild, we were greeted at a very early hour in the morn with the cry: an american *cartele Flagg*, flying in the harbour.* We went soon into the Town & learned that a ship had indeed arrived during the previous night

---

*Cartile. An agreement between enemies for the exchange of prisoners, according to Mr. Paine in the first edition of Cobb's memoir.

under the command of an american officer with a cartile flag. The officer had then gone to report himself to the port Admiral.

We forthwith repaired to a noted Coffee house, where the American officer soon arrived. Altho we were all strangers, he cordially shook us by the hand as americans and told us that he was 2d Leut. of the American Frigate *Essex*, Capt. Porter. The ship in the harbour was the British Sloop of War *Elert*, prize to the *Essex*. She had been sent in by Capt. Porter with her officers & crew on board, to be exchanged for the same number of Americans.

"But," said the Leut., "I have cause to fear that I may be a prisiner with you, for I left the old Admiral in a violent rage." He had told Duckworth that he could not negotiate. His orders, from Capt. Porter, were to lay here 24 hours, & if the terms were not complied with, to proceed on to America with the Prise & her Crew "or be your prisinner," said he, "as I'm in your power."

However, in a few minuits a note was received from the old Admiral, saying that upon a repe-rusual of Capt. Porter's dispatches, he found

The Essex capturing Alert.

that the *honor* of the *Elert*'s British officer was pledg'd for the fulfilling of the contract. He knew his government always Redeem'd the pledges of their officers, thus he wou'd receive the officers & crew of *Elert* and wou'd give in exchange, every American prissoner in port (and there were 2 to 1). We must be off in 24 hours.

Now, commenced a Scene of confusion and bussle. The Crew of the cartile was soon landed, and the Americans as speedily took possession of the *Elert*. The next morn at about the suns rising, we weighed her anchors and left the harbour of St. Johns, and made sail for New York with 246 Americans onboard.

We came along without falling in with any float-ing object, untill we were in the Longitude of the South shoal of Nantucket when we saw a topsail Schooner running off S. Easterly, upon which we fired & brought her to. She hoisted Sweedish colours, & lay bye untill we boarded her. We found she was out of Boston, bound for the West Indies, and gave us the pleasing account of the American Frigate, *Constitution,* having captured the British Frigate, *Garreire.*

This intilligence was communicated to the *Elert* by the boarding officer, and in quick time her yards were manned & three cheers were given, which might have been heard miles.

Two days after, we arrived in New York, and dispersed to our several places of residence. I took passage in a Schooner for Bass River, with my two mates & Josiah Crosby, brother to the lad I had sent home earlier. We reached the river at about the sunsetting, & being but about 6 miles from my family, I could not sleep without seeing them. Consequently myself, & my 1st. mate, *Mr. Berry*, each hired a Saddle horse & started for Brewster.

It may perhaps amuse you, my dear G. Childen, if I turn back to the time of my arrival at St. Johns. Do you remember that the Port Admiral, Sir J. T. Duckworth, had given liberty to the American Supercargoes & passengers to purchase a vessel & git home at their own expence? And that I obtained liberty to send the Crosby boy home by this conveyance, petitioning the Admiral, applying pritty strongly to the old Gentlemans feelings, untill he ageed to send him home to his parents. This gave me an oppertunity to inform my Family of my capture and send some money home, as well as grattifing my relatives by sending home their beloved son. The dear child wore the money in a kerchief around his neck, and delivered it, along with my letter, to his aunt [his aunt being my beloved wife].

Now, as it happened, the Crosby lad delivered my letter and the money at about 8 o'clock the same evening I arrived at Bass river and set out for Brewster. I reached my dwelling & gave a knock at your G. Mother's sleeping room winder at about 12 o'clock.

It appears she had been reperusing my Lengthy letter, Imigining & revolving in mind all the horrors of my situation in an English prisin *after she had been in bed,* & had not been asleep when I knok'd at the Window.

"Who is there?" said she.

"It is I," said I.

"Well, what do you want?"

"To come in."

"For what?" said she.

Before I cou'd answer I heard my daughter, who was in bed with her say:

"Why, *Mar, it's Par!*"

This was eneogh. The doors flew open, and the greetings of affection & consanguinity miltiplied upon me rapidly. Thus, in a moment I was transported to the greatest earthly bliss a man can have, viz to the enjoyment of the happy family circil.

THE END

Made in the USA
Monee, IL
17 November 2025

35103069R00073